The Night Before Christmas

Clement C. Moore

Mark Marshall

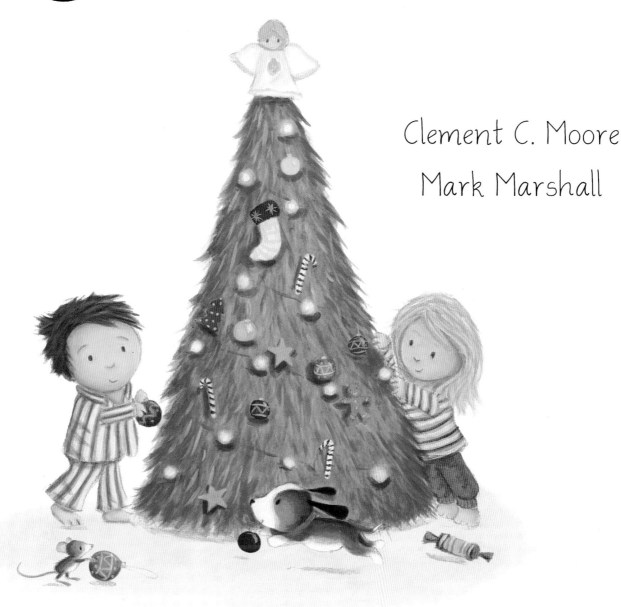

LITTLE TIGER PRESS
London

'Twas the night before Christmas,
when all through the house
Not a creature was stirring,
not even a mouse.

The stockings were hung
by the chimney with care,
In hopes that
St Nicholas
soon would be there.

Us children were nestled
all snug in our beds,
While visions of
s u g a r - p l u m s
danced in our heads.

And Mamma in her 'kerchief, and Dada in his cap,
Had just settled down for a long winter's nap.

When out on the lawn
there arose such a
c l a t t e r,
I sprang from the bed
to see what was the matter.

Away to the window
I flew like a flash,
Tore open the shutters
and threw up the sash.

The moon on the breast of the new-fallen snow
Gave the lustre of mid-day to objects below.
When, what to my wondering eyes should appear,
But a miniature sleigh, and eight tiny reindeer.

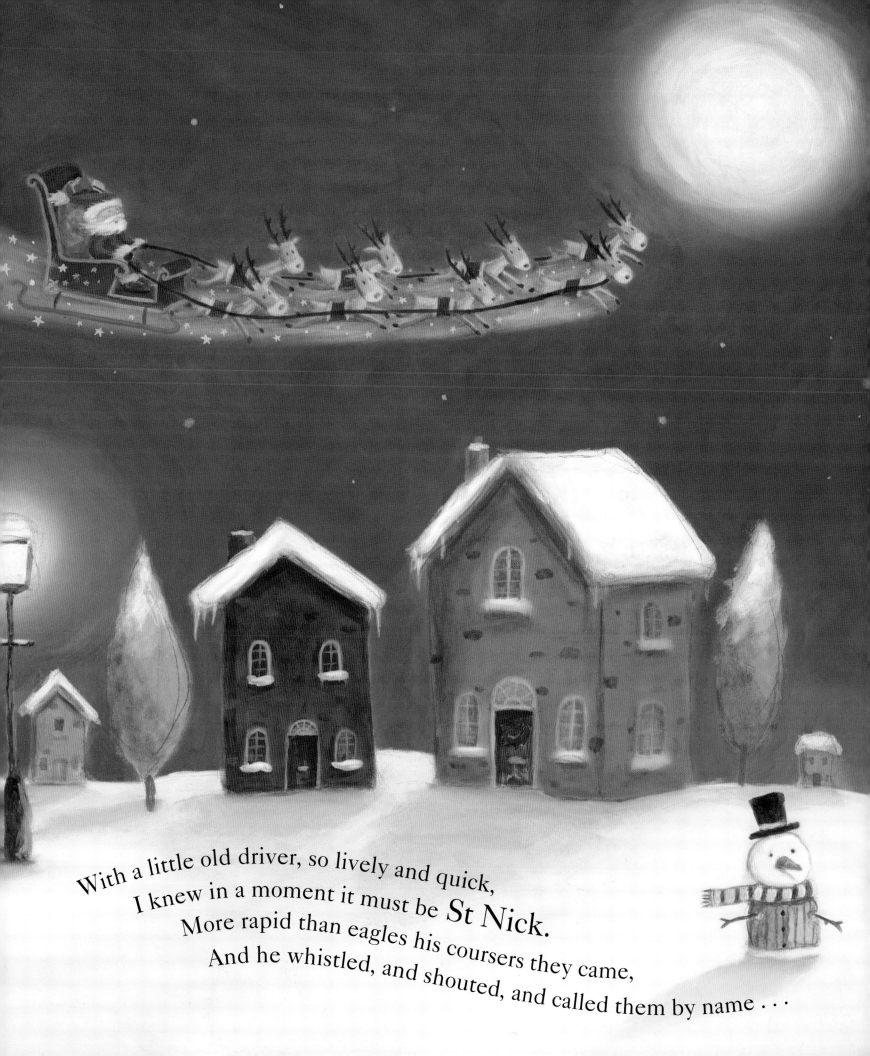

With a little old driver, so lively and quick,
I knew in a moment it must be St Nick.
More rapid than eagles his coursers they came,
And he whistled, and shouted, and called them by name . . .

"Now Dasher,
now Dancer, now Prancer,
and Vixen!
On Comet, on Cupid, on Donder
and Blitzen!

To the top of the porch,
to the top of the wall!
Now dash away, dash away,
dash away all!"

As dry leaves that before
the wild hurricane fly,
When they meet with an obstacle,
mount to the sky,

So up to the house top
the coursers they flew,
With the sleigh full of toys,
and St Nicholas too.

And then, in a twinkling, I heard on the roof
The **prancing** and **pawing** of each **little hoof**.

As I drew in my head, and was turning around,
Down the chimney St Nicholas came with a bound.

He was dressed all in fur, from his head to his foot,
And his clothes were all tarnished with ashes and soot.
A bundle of toys he had flung on his back,
And he looked like a peddler just opening his pack.

His eyes – how they twinkled! His dimples how merry!
His cheeks were like roses, his nose like a cherry!
His droll little mouth was drawn up like a bow,
And the beard of his chin was as white as the snow.

The stump of a pipe he held tight in his teeth,
And the smoke it encircled his head like a wreath.
He had a broad face, and a little round belly,
That shook when he laughed like a bowlful of jelly.

He was chubby and plump,
a right jolly old elf,
And I laughed when I saw him,
in spite of myself.

A wink of his eye
and a twist of his head,
Soon gave me to know
I had nothing to dread.

He spoke not a word,
but went straight to his work,
And filled all the stockings,
then turned with a jerk.

And laying his finger
aside of his nose,
And giving a nod,
up the chimney
he rose.

He sprang to his sleigh, to his team gave a whistle,

And away they all flew like the down of a thistle.

But I heard him exclaim, 'ere he drove out of sight,

"*Happy Christmas* to all, and to all a good night!*"